T0327166

PRAYERS OF THE OLD TESTAMENT

LYNNE M. BAAB

8 STUDIES
FOR INDIVIDUALS
OR GROUPS

Life
Builder
Study

INTER-VARSITY PRESS
36 Causton Street, London SW1P 4ST, England
Email: ivp@ivpbooks.com
Website: www.ivpbooks.com

*Originally published in the United States of America in the LifeGuide® Bible Studies series
in 2010 by InterVarsity Press, Downers Grove, Illinois
First published in Great Britain by Scripture Union in 2011
This edition published in Great Britain by Inter-Varsity Press 2019*

British Library Cataloguing-in-Publication Data
A catalogue record for this book is available from the British Library.

ISBN: 978–1–78359–835–9

Printed in Great Britain by Ashford Colour Press Ltd, Gosport, Hampshire

Contents

Getting the Most Out of
Prayers of the Old Testament

The Psalms are often called the prayer book of the Bible, and they provide beautiful models for a variety of moods and aspects of prayer. Throughout the ages, Christians have memorized the Psalms, praised God in communal worship with the Psalms and poured out their hearts to God using the emotive words of the Psalms.

Many Christians don't realize that dozens of prayers that are equally rich can be found elsewhere in the Bible. Some of the briefest prayers are evocative and inspiring, such as Samuel's prayer as a boy: "Speak, for your servant is listening" (1 Samuel 3:10). Some are exuberant and joyful, such as Moses' and Miriam's prayers of exultation after God parted the Red Sea (Exodus 15:1-21). Jeremiah's prayers resonate with honest passion and pain, expressing his need for God in powerful and vivid language.

Each of the prayers in the Bible provides a model for our own prayers—as individuals, in small group settings and in corporate worship—which can help us get out of our ruts. Many of us tend to pray for the same things over and over: the same requests for our loved ones and the same pleas for the difficulties in our own lives. Similarly, when we focus our prayers on gratitude, we tend to praise and thank God for the same kinds of things. The prayers we'll study from the Old Testament can teach us to pray in new ways, bringing freshness to our routines. In many cases, we can even use the exact words of a prayer in the Bible.

These prayers also show diverse moods and expressions of prayer. They demonstrate that a variety of emotions can play a role in calling us into God's presence, and they provide answers to some common questions: Can I be honest with God in prayer? Can I truly bring all my emotions before God as I pray? Does God really care about everything in my life? Does God really enter into every part of my life?

How can we know that a section of Scripture is a prayer? Some passages tell us in very clear terms that the person is praying: "From inside the fish, Jonah prayed to the LORD his God. He said . . ." (Jonah 2:1-2). Many of the prayers in this study guide follow that pattern. However, in other cases we have to discern that a passage of Scripture is a prayer. Several times in the book of Jeremiah, for example, the prophet simply begins to address God: "You are always righteous, O LORD, when I bring a case before you" (Jeremiah 12:1).

The eight prayers in this study guide all address God directly for at least part of the prayer. However, several of them also include sections that describe God using third-person language. For example, Habakkuk's prayer moves back and forth between addressing God using "you" and talking about God and what God has done. Because of that back-and-forth movement, I consider all of Habakkuk 3 to be a prayer, even though all of it does not address God directly. These prayers that alternate between addressing God directly and talking about God are similar to today's praise songs, many of which make the same back-and-forth movement.

These prayers are a rich resource to help us deepen our prayers. As you study them, consider using them as your own prayers when the mood and timing are appropriate. You may want to memorize one or more of them so you can pray the words as you lie in bed at night or as you wait at a stoplight. You may also want to rewrite one or more of the prayers to fit the circumstances of your life, using some of the vocabulary and the main ideas in the biblical prayer.

The prayers in this guide present God as powerful and majestic, the Creator of all and the Lord of all. They also help us see God as the One who saves his people from disaster, and the One who listens and cares when his people are in need. What a privilege to know this God, both mighty and gentle, and to be invited into prayer.

Suggestions for Individual Study

1. As you begin each study, pray that God will speak to you through his Word.

2. Read the introduction to the study and respond to the personal reflection question or exercise. This is designed to help you focus on

God and on the theme of the study.

3. Each study deals with a particular passage so that you can delve into the author's meaning in that context. Read and reread the passage to be studied. The questions are written using the language of the New International Version, so you may wish to use that version of the Bible. The New Revised Standard Version is also recommended.

4. This is an inductive Bible study, designed to help you discover for yourself what Scripture is saying. The study includes three types of questions. *Observation* questions ask about the basic facts: who, what, when, where and how. *Interpretation* questions delve into the meaning of the passage. *Application* questions help you discover the implications of the text for growing in Christ. These three keys unlock the treasures of Scripture.

Write your answers to the questions in the spaces provided or in a personal journal. Writing can bring clarity and deeper understanding of yourself and of God's Word.

5. It might be good to have a Bible dictionary handy. Use it to look up any unfamiliar words, names or places.

6. Use the prayer suggestion to guide you in thanking God for what you have learned and to pray about the applications that have come to mind.

7. You may want to go on to the suggestion under "Now or Later," or you may want to use that idea for your next study.

Suggestions for Members of a Group Study

1. Come to the study prepared. Follow the suggestions for individual study mentioned above. You will find that careful preparation will greatly enrich your time spent in group discussion.

2. Be willing to participate in the discussion. The leader of your group will not be lecturing. Instead, he or she will be encouraging the members of the group to discuss what they have learned. The leader will be asking the questions that are found in this guide.

3. Stick to the topic being discussed. Your answers should be based on the verses which are the focus of the discussion and not on outside authorities such as commentaries or speakers. These studies focus on a particular passage of Scripture. Only rarely should you refer to

other portions of the Bible. This allows for everyone to participate in in-depth study on equal ground.

4. Be sensitive to the other members of the group. Listen attentively when they describe what they have learned. You may be surprised by their insights! Each question assumes a variety of answers. Many questions do not have "right" answers, particularly questions that aim at meaning or application. Instead the questions push us to explore the passage more thoroughly.

When possible, link what you say to the comments of others. Also, be affirming whenever you can. This will encourage some of the more hesitant members of the group to participate.

5. Be careful not to dominate the discussion. We are sometimes so eager to express our thoughts that we leave too little opportunity for others to respond. By all means participate! But allow others to also.

6. Expect God to teach you through the passage being discussed and through the other members of the group. Pray that you will have an enjoyable and profitable time together, but also that as a result of the study you will find ways that you can take action individually and/or as a group.

7. Remember that anything said in the group is considered confidential and should not be discussed outside the group unless specific permission is given to do so.

8. If you are the group leader, you will find additional suggestions at the back of the guide.

1

A Prayer of Moses

Praising God for Doing Wonders

My husband tells me that I have a certain smile that he has seen only a few times at very significant occasions. He saw it for the first time on our wedding day. With this smile, my face radiates absolute joy and exuberant happiness, as if my heart is so full that my face must shine with it.

I'd like to believe that particular smile would have been on my face if I'd been present with the Israelites after they walked through the Red Sea. The Israelites had been in slavery in Egypt for many generations, working long days at backbreaking labor with no sabbath day for rest. Their despair was absolute until Moses came on the scene. God raised up Moses as a leader to confront Pharaoh, and the Israelites probably began to have a small amount of hope. Then the plagues God sent on Egypt likely created both confusion and cautious optimism among the people of Israel. Was God going to save them? After the plagues, Pharaoh let the Israelites go. Finally they were on their way to freedom!

But then they saw Pharaoh's armies pursuing them. Their optimism undoubtedly flew away in the face of terror. However, God split the waters of the Red Sea for them to cross and then closed those waters again after them, killing their enemies. After all those up and down emotions, the exuberance of deliverance must have been in-toxicating. I bet many people were smiling with great joy.

GROUP DISCUSSION. Have you ever experienced great joy after a tu-mult of painful and powerful emotions? What was it like? What did it feel like in your body? In what ways did God's presence seem real?

PERSONAL REFLECTION. Spend some time reflecting on times of strong emotion in your life. Where is God in those feelings? In what ways are you able to turn to God in times of strong emotions? In what ways would you like to?

After the crossing of the Red Sea, Moses leads the people of Israel in a prayer of great praise. *Read Exodus 15:1-18.*

1. Verses 1-10 describe God's actions using many powerful verbs. List the verbs that seem most vivid to you.

2. In verse 2, Moses calls the Lord "my strength," "my song" and "my salvation." What do you think Moses means by each name?

Which of these characteristics of God have you experienced most strongly? Explain the circumstances.

3. Verses 5 to 10 frequently evoke God as the Creator and the Lord of creation. Describe the references to nature in these verses.

Do these verses change your view of God at all? If so, how?

---

4. In verse 11, Moses focuses on God's holiness, glory and wonders. Why do you think Moses zeroes in on these three characteristics of God?

---

5. In verse 11 Moses introduces the idea that Israel's God is unique among the gods. What do we learn in verses 12 to 18 that illustrates the uniqueness of Israel's God?

---

6. Contrast the emotions and situations of the redeemed people in verses 11 to 13 with those of the nations in verses 14 to 16.

What attitudes toward God have you seen from others today, and how do you think those different attitudes in people develop?

7. In what ways does God's tender care for the people of Israel, described in verses 13 and 17, complement the picture of God as a warrior from verse 3?

8. How have you experienced God fighting for you (as a warrior) when you have been in deep need?

How have you experienced God's tender care?

9. The prayer opens with the words, "I will sing to the LORD." In what ways does music help you praise and thank God?

10. In order to praise and thank God when we pray, we need to remember what God has done. What is one practice you can implement that will help you regularly look back and remember God's actions in your life?

Spend some time praising and thanking God for the ways he has worked in your life in the past week.

Now or Later

This study guide presents an opportunity to grow and develop your own prayer practices. As you begin this study guide, spend some time reflecting on, journaling about, or discussing your desires and dreams for your prayer life. What do you like about the way you now pray, both alone and with others? What aspects of your current prayer life are not satisfying? In what ways would you like to grow in prayer? Pray about the role of prayer in your life, confessing your shortcomings to God, asking for God's guidance for ways to grow in prayer and telling God your dreams for your prayer life.

Read Psalm 29, a psalm that uses an extended metaphor of a storm to describe God's power, majesty and glory. Compare and contrast the psalm with Moses' prayer. After you have compared the two texts, read Psalm 29 a second time slowly, praying the words as you read them.

2

A Prayer of Hannah

Turning Things Upside Down

1 Samuel 2:1-10

Right after Nat and Marlene got married, Marlene got cancer. Luckily it was treatable, but the radiation that cured the cancer resulted in infertility. Marlene and Nat longed to have children, so after much prayer and discussion with friends, they decided to adopt. And after many long and tortuous steps, they were able to adopt two babies, a boy and a girl. Their children are now in elementary school. They thank God daily that they've been able to parent their two beautiful children.

GROUP DISCUSSION. On a piece of paper make a list of things you have prayed for that seemed impossible or that still seem impossible. Put a check mark by any of the prayers that have been answered in any way at all. Describe one thing on your list to the group.

PERSONAL REFLECTION. What are the areas of your life that are hardest for you to pray for? Spend some time reflecting on why it's hard to pray for those aspects of your life. Write out a prayer, asking God to teach you how to pray for those things.

Hannah had a similar experience. She longed for children but didn't get pregnant for a long time after her marriage. During a yearly festival, Hannah prayed in the sanctuary at Shiloh, pouring out her heart to God in prayer. She promised God that if she had a son, she would give him back to the Lord. The priest, Eli, promised her that her prayer would be answered. Her son was born, and she named him Samuel. When he was weaned, she brought him to the temple at Shiloh, to be trained by Eli. After Hannah left her miracle child, Samuel, with Eli, she prayed a remarkable prayer. *Read 1 Samuel 2:1-10.*

---

1. Name the characteristics of God that are mentioned in verses 1 to 3. Why would these characteristics be significant to Hannah?

---

2. Which of the characteristics of God in verses 1 to 3 is most important to you today? Why?

---

3. This prayer addresses God directly only twice (at the end of v. 1 and beginning of v. 2). Who do you think the rest of the prayer addresses?

---

4. Verses 4 to 8 list unexpected outcomes that result from God's intervention. What does this list reveal about God?

5. When have you seen God perform reverses like the ones described in verses 4 to 8?

---

6. Hannah's prayer focuses on people in need and people on the margins of society. In what ways is Hannah herself marginalized?

What do you learn from Hannah's prayer that might help you pray for yourself in a different way?

---

7. Are there any actions you can take to participate in God's work of helping the marginalized and working for reversals of seemingly impossible situations?

---

8. List the promises described in verses 9 and 10. What did they mean for Hannah?

for Israel?

What do they mean in our context today? Sit in silence for a few minutes to let the reality of those promises sink into your mind and heart.

9. The words at the end of verse 9, "it is not by strength that one prevails," could be viewed as the main point of Hannah's prayer. How does this brief statement sum up the ideas in the prayer?

10. In this prayer, God is portrayed as all-powerful and also willing to enter into our broken world. What does this combination mean to you?

11. Hannah is praying in the midst of a deeply personal family drama, yet her prayer expresses concern for the larger world; she mentions warriors, princes, the powerful, the poor, the hungry. How closely do your prayers and your faith in God's power and care model hers in this way? Why do you think that is?

Spend some time praying that God would give you the imagination to pray for the kinds of reversals that honor God.

Now or Later

Mary's prayer in Luke 1:46-55 contains many of the same themes as Hannah's prayer. Read Mary's prayer, watching for comparisons and contrasts with Hannah's prayer. After you have spent some time comparing and contrasting the two prayers, read the words of Mary's prayer slowly, praying them as you read them.

Psalm 113 is another passage with many parallels to Hannah's prayer. Compare and contrast the psalm with Hannah's prayer. Then read the psalm slowly, using the words of the psalm as your own prayer.

3

A Prayer of Samuel

Learning to Listen

1 Samuel 3:1-14

I've made a lot of jokes about my wish that God would write answers to my questions in the sky. When I'm trying to make a hard decision between two equally sensible options, or when I can't think of any possible solutions to a problem, I often say, "I wish that God would hire one of those cute little airplanes that write messages in the sky and tell me exactly what to do."

As I've matured as a Christian, however, I've learned to discern God's voice more readily, and I've experienced his voice more frequently. God speaks to me through Scripture, songs, sermons and other people and in a still small voice as I pray. Sometimes his voice gives me the profound encouragement that I am loved. Other times God's voice tells me to do something, most often to reach out to someone in need.

Whatever I sense him saying, God's voice almost always surprises me, calling me to do things I wasn't even thinking about or to believe I'm loved at the times when I feel most unlovable. I have found that the more I obey God's voice when I hear it, the more often I hear it. I'm still waiting for God to sky-write answers to my questions, but I take comfort in Jesus' words that his sheep recognize his voice and listen to it (John 10:27).

GROUP DISCUSSION. Do you think there are things we can do to make it more likely that God will speak to us? What might those things be? What are the obstacles to believing God can speak to us?

PERSONAL REFLECTION. Write a prayer about your desire for God to speak to you. In the prayer try to acknowledge to God the reasons why you might want him to speak to you and the reasons why you might not want him to speak, and offer both up to him.

God speaks to Samuel (Hannah's son), and his mentor, Eli, has to teach him how to respond. *Read 1 Samuel 3:1-14.*

1. What emotions do you think Samuel experienced throughout the night?

2. From verses 1-3 and 11-14, what do you think the spiritual issues were while Eli was the priest in the temple at Shiloh?

3. Eli is Samuel's teacher and mentor. Who are the people who taught you about God when you were a child or teenager?

4. What are all the facts we know about when and where this incident took place (vv. 2 and 3)?

5. In verses 4 to 10, why do you think Samuel has difficulty recognizing that it is God who is speaking to him?

6. What do you think are the difficulties for people today in hearing God speak to them?

7. What do you learn about the relationship between Samuel and Eli in this exchange?

Despite Eli's failings as a father, in what ways is he a good mentor to Samuel?

8. What do you think is significant about the words Eli instructs Samuel to say to God (v. 9)?

9. Do you think Samuel is surprised at the words God speaks to him (vv. 11-14)? Why or why not?

10. Have you ever been surprised by something you sensed God saying to you? If so, what did he say, and why were you surprised?

Are there places in your life where you are more receptive to God's truth or more likely to hear God's voice speaking to you? If so, explain.

---

11. Samuel used the words "Speak, for your servant is listening" to express his willingness to hear and obey God. What words might you use to express your desire to hear God's voice and your willingness to obey what you hear?

Spend some time praying about your willingness to hear God speak and to obey what you hear.

Now or Later

Perhaps there are areas of your life that you cannot imagine God caring about, or perhaps there are places in your life that you cannot imagine God entering into. Read Psalm 139:1-16 and imagine God speaking into every area of your life.

Read Psalm 145:18 and spend some time rejoicing in God's nearness and pondering what it means to call on God "in truth."

4

A Prayer of Solomon

Interceding for the Nations

1 Kings 8:22-53

Sometimes I like to picture the people in my life as if they are positioned in a series of concentric circles. One circle, closest to me, contains my nuclear family and my closest friends. A second circle, just outside the first one, contains my extended family members, work colleagues and additional friends. In the next circle are acquaintances. In the next circle are the citizens of my town, and the next circle contains the people who live in my country. The outermost circle holds all the people in the world.

I like to meditate on God's love for the people in each of those circles. I may feel more love for the people in the circles closest to me, but God's love overflows into all the circles. I find it challenging to evaluate my prayer life in the light of all these concentric circles. Do I pray for people in each of the circles? Or do all my intercessory prayers focus on one or two of the circles?

GROUP DISCUSSION. If you were going to pray a public prayer for the people in your nation and other nations as well, what topics would you include in your prayer? Why would you choose those topics?

PERSONAL REFLECTION. Imagine that you have been asked to pray a public prayer at the dedication of an important building in your community, such as the city hall, a public library or a sports center. Write out the words that you would pray.

We get a glimpse of God's concern for all peoples of the earth in King Solomon's passionate prayer at the time of the dedication of the temple in Jerusalem. Solomon's father, David, wanted to build a temple for God, but God forbade him to do so, telling David that Solomon would be the one to build it. Solomon's temple was lavishly decorated with the finest materials available. His prayer at the dedication shows that the passion of his heart for the temple didn't reside in the expensive materials. Instead, he longed for the temple to be a place of prayer for the people of Israel and for visitors and foreigners as well, a place where anyone could pray and God would answer. *Read 1 Kings 8:22-53.*

---

1. What attributes and characteristics of God stand out to you most from Solomon's prayer?

Based on his prayer, what stands out to you about Solomon's character?

---

2. In verses 23 to 26 God's promises and covenant are mentioned several times. What is the connection between God's promises and prayer?

3. In verses 27 to 29, the question of where God dwells comes up several times. Where do you believe he dwells?

How do you think your belief about where he dwells affects your relationship with him?

4. List the words Solomon uses synonymously for the word *prayer* in verses 28 to 30. What different aspects of prayer are revealed by these words?

5. In verses 31 to 40, Solomon prays for four specific situations, each one introduced by the word *when*. Summarize these four requests. If you could choose one of these prayers to pray for situations today, which one would you pick and why?

6. In verses 41 to 43, Solomon prays for foreigners. How do you think he feels about foreigners coming to the temple?

7. What reasons does Solomon give about why he wants God to answer his prayer for foreigners in verses 41 to 43?

8. Based on verses 46 to 51, what are the steps involved in repentance?

———————————————————————

9. In verses 52 and 53, Solomon uses the word *servant* twice. What is the significance of Solomon calling Moses and himself God's servants as he concludes this prayer?

———————————————————————

10. How is Solomon's prayer a good model for the kind of prayer a servant leader might pray for the people he or she leads?

Who are the people God might be calling you to pray for along these lines as you serve or lead them?

———————————————————————

11. Think of some of the major contemporary needs of people around the world. What are several things you could pray for?

Spend some time praying for your nation and for people in other countries.

Now or Later

Earlier in his life, Solomon prayed for something that changed his life. Read 1 Kings 3:1-15 and notice why it was important for Solomon to build the temple. Also note what Solomon prays for and how God answers. Write your own prayer asking God to give you wisdom.

Psalm 96 expresses God's care for and his lordship over all the nations of the earth. Read the psalm, counting the references to the world's nations and peoples. Notice any parallels with Solomon's prayer. Then read the psalm again slowly, making the words your own prayer.

5

A Prayer of Isaiah

Confessing and Commissioning

Isaiah 6

I can remember a handful of times in my life when I have been overcome with awe and wonder. The first time it happened I was fourteen years old, standing in front of Michelangelo's *Pietà*. I was stunned by the powerful emotion conveyed by the white marble representation of Jesus after the crucifixion, in his mother's arms. I was so emotionally moved that my body froze in place.

The most recent time it happened, I was at the Grand Canyon with a friend who knows the Grand Canyon well. She took me to three different overlooks, all of them swarming with tourists. Then we went to a campsite she knew about, deserted that day. We parked the car and walked several hundred yards to the rim of the canyon. We sat on a big rock, all by ourselves, right on the edge of the canyon, and watched the sun set.

I can't begin to describe the splendor of that experience. The vivid sky, the red rocks, the depth of the canyon, and the scale of the whole thing . . . Stunning. Overwhelming. So beautiful it made my heart ache. It was a powerful reflection of the One who created it.

GROUP DISCUSSION. Can you remember a time when you felt awe and wonder? What did you see, hear, smell, taste or touch? Did you physically respond in some way, and if so, how?

PERSONAL REFLECTION. Reflect on what happens in your body when you experience awe and wonder. What parts of your body are affected? In what ways is it a comfortable experience? In what ways is it uncomfortable?

I know my moments of awe and wonder are small and incomplete compared to Isaiah's encounter with God. My experiences give me just a small glimpse of what Isaiah must have felt. *Read Isaiah 6.*

1. Would you like to experience a vision of God like this one? Why or why not?

2. Why do you think it matters what year this incident happened?

3. Verses 1 to 4 set the scene. If you were there with Isaiah, what would you see, hear, smell, taste or feel in your body?

What aspects of the character of God are communicated in those verses?

4. What adjectives would you use to describe the way Isaiah feels in verse 5?

5. In verse 5 Isaiah says, "I am a man of unclean lips, and I live among a people of unclean lips." What do you think is the significance of lips?

6. Verse 8 is the first time God speaks in this passage. Do you think it is necessary to have guilt taken away in order to hear God's voice? Why or why not?

7. What do you think motivates Isaiah to say that he is willing to be sent, despite the fact that he doesn't know anything about his task when he volunteers?

8. Have you ever volunteered for something without knowing exactly what would be involved? If so, why did you volunteer?

9. What might have surprised Isaiah about God's words in verses 9 to 13?

10. What emotions do you think Isaiah experienced once he heard what God wanted him to do?

_____

11. The glimmer of hope in these words from God comes in the last line of verse 13. What do you think Isaiah means by "the holy seed"?

_____

12. Look back over the sequence of events in this passage: a vision of God, repentance, receiving forgiveness, being willing to go and serve, and then receiving a commission from God. In your own life, have you ever experienced connections between any of these same kinds of events?

_____

13. If God came to you as he did to Isaiah, and you wanted to express your willingness to obey, what words might you use?

Spend some time confessing your sins, either silently or out loud. Then pray that God would help you hear his voice about where and how to serve, and that he would give you a willing heart to act on what you hear.

Now or Later

The first chapter of Jeremiah records Jeremiah's call to be a prophet. His call has numerous similarities with Isaiah's call. Read Jeremiah

1:1-10, looking for the similarities with Isaiah 6. Imagine yourself in Jeremiah's place. What would you say to God? Reflect on times when God has called you to do something. What did you learn from those experiences? Is God calling you to do anything right now?

Psalm 8 expresses some of the same awe at God's greatness that Isaiah experienced, and the psalm also describes the high calling of humans as God's agents on earth. Read Psalm 8 two times, the first time to notice comparisons with Isaiah 6. The second time you read it, read slowly and pray the words to indicate your awe at God's greatness, coupled with your willingness to be faithful to God's call.

6

A Prayer of Jeremiah

Bringing Every Emotion to God

I struggled with depression off and on for sixteen years. The book of Jeremiah, and particularly his prayers, provided many moments of solace for me. Jeremiah was honest with God about how he felt, expressing his deep sadness, pain and anger that God had called him to prophesy news of destruction and judgment to the people of Israel. Jeremiah's powerful emotions came in part from the content of the message, but his pain and anger also came from the response of the people as he prophesied the message from God. Jeremiah was laughed at, mocked and imprisoned because of the message God gave him to speak. Yet he never stopped obeying God, and he never stopped telling God how much it hurt to obey him.

In the midst of my own dark days, Jeremiah encouraged me to continue to pray. Jeremiah helped me see that it is a thousand times better to bring our anger, frustration and pain to God than try to cope with it on our own. When we bring negative emotions to God in prayer, God works in us, teaching us patience and perseverance, shaping us into Christ's likeness. In the end, praying our way through hard times gives us joy. That joy may not come quickly, but it definitely comes in the end.

I'm grateful that my dark days are largely in the past and that joy is a major part of my life today. However, discouragement, anger, sorrow and sadness play a role in almost everyone's life from time to time, and Jeremiah can be a wonderful encouragement to bring every emotion to God, no matter how much pain we are feeling.

GROUP DISCUSSION. Think of a situation when you were able to express a negative emotion to God in prayer and received help with that negative emotion. Or think of a time when you wished you could pray about something difficult in your life but were afraid to be honest with God.

PERSONAL REFLECTION. Spend some time thinking about the role of positive and negative emotions in your family of origin. Which emotions were acceptable and unacceptable to express? Do you see any carryover of the patterns from your family of origin into your prayer life today? Write out a prayer about emotions and prayer, thanking God for his willingness to hear you no matter what you are feeling and asking God to help you grow in bringing every emotion to him.

Jeremiah 20 records a twenty-four-hour period in Jeremiah's life when he is imprisoned in stocks, speaks out about the person who imprisoned him and then prays about the incident. *Read Jeremiah 20.*

1. Jeremiah 20 is like a three-act play (vv. 1-2, 3-6 and 7-18). Give a brief title for each of the three acts.

2. Imagine being wrongly punished or imprisoned. What range of emotions might you experience?

3. Jeremiah's words to Pashhur in verses 4 to 6 were typical of his prophecies about the coming destruction of Judah. Summarize Jeremiah's prophecy. What is the significance of the repetition of the word *all?*

4. In verses 7 to 10, Jeremiah expresses to God his frustration and pain. What is his dilemma?

5. Have you or people you know ever obeyed God and experienced unexpected troubles or problems as a result? If so, what happened?

How did the experience change your (or their) relationship with God?

6. In verses 11 to 13, Jeremiah's tone shifts dramatically. What characteristics of God does he highlight in these verses?

Why might these characteristics be significant to Jeremiah in his situation?

7. Go back over the entire prayer—verses 7 to 18—and list every emotion you can think of that might lie behind the words Jeremiah says.

---

8. To whom is it easiest for you to express emotion? Why?

What emotions are easiest and hardest for you to express?

---

9. Do you believe God invites you to express all those emotions to him in prayer? How did that belief develop in you?

What benefits do you think can come from expressing every emotion to God in prayer?

---

10. What are some practices that could help you grow in speaking honestly to God?

Spend some time praying that God would teach you how to grow in being honest with him in prayer.

Now or Later

Jeremiah 12:1-4 and 15:15-18 are two other prayers of Jeremiah. Read them and watch for emotions similar to and different from those expressed in Jeremiah 20. Also look for the balance of honest expression of feelings and statements of trust in God. In these two additional prayers, what can you learn from Jeremiah's honesty about his pain and anger coupled with his trust in God's goodness and power? If your emotions in any way mirror Jeremiah's emotions, read his words again slowly as a prayer. You may also want to pray Jeremiah's words for someone you know who is feeling the same emotions as Jeremiah.

Psalms 42 and 43 appear to belong together because they have the same format. These two psalms contain many of the same emotions as Jeremiah's prayers. Compare and contrast these psalms with Jeremiah's prayers. Then read Psalms 42 and 43 again slowly, praying the words for yourself or praying them for someone you know who is discouraged or depressed.

7

A Prayer of Jonah

Praying in Desperate Situations

Jonah 2

I was driving a group of students to a retreat in the mountains in my big, old car. As we turned off the main road in the dark, I tried to drive very carefully, because the gravel road was covered with snow. We came to a small stream with a narrow, wooden, snow-covered bridge over it, with no side railings. I drove even more slowly but still the car slid sideways, and the right front wheel went over the edge of the bridge. The car tilted to rest on its undercarriage.

Gingerly, we got out of the car to survey the situation. Someone suggested that we pray for God's help, so we stood there in the cold night, praying. After the prayer, someone else suggested that we try to lift the car back onto the bridge, and we did. None of us were particularly athletic, big or strong, and I still don't know how we did it. It felt like a miracle of God's deliverance then, and, many years later, it still stays in my memory that way.

GROUP DISCUSSION. Have you ever experienced a situation where God delivered you? Did prayer play a role in it? If so, what did you pray?

PERSONAL REFLECTION. The saying that originated in World War II—"There are no atheists in foxholes"—refers to the idea that in times of great danger, people may be likely to turn to God in prayer, perhaps in a different way than they do in ordinary life. Is that true for you? Are your prayers different in times of danger or stress and, if so, in what ways? What beliefs about God are triggered for you in times of great need?

The story of Jonah is probably one of the most well-known Bible stories. Jonah ran away from God, ended up in the belly of a whale or fish, and survived. Even though the story is familiar, few people are familiar with Jonah's prayer from inside the fish; it's a remarkable statement of faith in God's power to deliver us from danger and disaster. *Read Jonah 2.*

1. If Jonah 2 were rewritten in the form of a play, there would be three main actors: God, Jonah and the water. What actions are attributed to each of the three?

2. Verse 2 functions like an overview expressing the central focus of Jonah's prayer. What do you notice about the verb tenses in verse 2?

What do you think is the significance of speaking God's deliverance while still in the midst of a crisis?

3. What does it mean to you that God answers you and listens to your cry?

4. In verses 3 to 6, Jonah lays out the situation in which he finds himself. Summarize his situation. What metaphors and images does he use?

Have you ever faced a situation that felt as overwhelming and threatening to you as Jonah's does to him? If so, what were the circumstances?

5. Verse 8 is a teaching maxim placed in the middle of the prayer. In what ways is it relevant to Jonah's situation?

6. What do you think are the common "worthless idols" of our time?

In what ways do these "worthless idols" cause us to forfeit God's grace?

7. Jonah uses "yet" or "but" three times in his prayer (vv. 4, 6 and 8-9). What contrast in circumstances or perspective does each verse describe?

What do the contrasts highlight about God's character?

8. Jonah's struggling ceases and he acknowledges that God is his salvation. What has helped you come to that place of changed perspective and deeper faith when you've faced overwhelming circumstances?

---

9. In what areas of your life do you find it hardest to trust that God will be your salvation?

In what current situation do you need help to see and believe that God is your salvation?

Spend some time praying for any hard situations you are facing and for willingness in each circumstance to wholly submit to God.

Now or Later

David's prayer in 2 Samuel 22:1-51 praises God for deliverance in much the same way that Jonah's does. Read David's prayer and compare and contrast the way these two prayers praise God for his power to save. After you have compared the two passages, read 2 Samuel 22 again slowly, making the words your own prayer.

Read Psalm 61:1-5, noticing the metaphors of rock, tower, tent and refuge. Think about the significance of those images of God's strength and goodness in times of trouble, and write your own prayer using the same metaphors.

8

A Prayer of Habakkuk

Trusting God in Spite of Circumstances

Habakkuk 3

Cho was alone at Christmastime. She couldn't make the long trip home, and no one from her family could come to visit her. She had begun to make friends with the other students, but they had all left to go home for the holiday. She felt very lonely, and anger welled up in her heart. God had led her so clearly to study in a foreign country, and now he had abandoned her at Christmastime.

Cho remembered all the people in the Bible who had poured out their feelings to God. She shut the curtains in her small apartment so no one would see her crying and then let out her anger in a storm of tears. She shook her fist at God as the tears poured down her face. "Why would you bring me here and then leave me alone? Do you love me at all? Where are you?" God answered her with a powerful sense of peace, security and companionship that filled the rest of her Christmas break.

GROUP DISCUSSION. Describe to the group the kinds of situations that make you feel angry.

PERSONAL REFLECTION. Have you ever expressed anger to God?

What kind of an answer did you hope for or expect? Did God answer you? In what ways did the process change your view of God?

Habakkuk was angry too. He was incredulous that God would allow his people, the Israelites, to pervert justice and harm the innocent. So he brought his anger to God, and God's answer—that the Babylonians would soon destroy the people of Israel—made him even more incredulous. The Babylonians were known throughout the world as a ruthless and fearsome people. Why would God use the Babylonians to discipline his own people? So Habakkuk questioned God again, and God answered again, showing Habakkuk that in time the Babylonians would reap what they had sown. In response, Habakkuk expressed his faith in God and his trust in God's ways. *Read Habakkuk 3.*

1. In verse 2, Habakkuk refers to God's fame and God's deeds. What hints from verses 2-15 give you an idea of what Habakkuk might have been thinking about?

2. What adjectives would you use to describe Habakkuk's vision in verses 3 to 15?

How comfortable or uncomfortable do you feel using these adjectives in relation to God? Why?

3. In describing what he saw of God, Habakkuk uses the words "glory" (v. 3) and "splendor" (v. 4) but also "rage" (v. 8) and "wrath" (vv. 8, 12). Explain how you think these can fit together and coexist.

4. In verse 16, what does Habakkuk's physical response say about the impact of this vision he has just seen?

5. In the second half of verse 16, Habakkuk says he will wait patiently. What do you think brings about his change of attitude from anger and confusion to a willingness to wait patiently and trust God?

6. In verses 17 and 18, Habakkuk says he will rejoice in the Lord even when things are horribly difficult. What are some of the things he expects to go wrong?

7. Paraphrase verses 17 and 18 for the twenty-first century, making them relevant to your life.

8. How is it possible for someone to rejoice in the Lord and be joyful in God, in a spirit of true honesty, in the midst of extremely difficult circumstances?

9. Verse 19 uses the metaphor of a deer. What does this metaphor communicate?

How easy or hard is it for you to believe God gives this kind of help in hard situations? Why?

---

10. Habakkuk's statement of trust follows his vision of God's power. When in your life have you seen God clearly enough for it to have an impact on the way you trust God?

---

11. What daily or weekly practices in your life have laid the ground-work for trusting God in difficult situations?

What practices might you adopt that would help you grow in trust?

Spend some time praying that God would enable you to see him clearly enough to be able to trust him in hard times.

Now or Later

Psalm 73 describes a similar journey to Habakkuk's. The psalmist is angry about the wickedness around him and can't seem to get over it until he enters the sanctuary of God. God speaks to him there, and the psalmist is able to express his trust in God's goodness and

God's justice. Read the psalm and think about what makes you angry. When you come to the statements of trust at the end of the psalm, see if you can pray the same words honestly and with integrity. If you can't, ask God to make those words of trust real in your life.

As you come to the end of this study guide, look back over the eight lessons. Spend some time reflecting on the ways these prayers from the Old Testament have encouraged you to grow in your own prayers. Make a list of the ways you would like to broaden your own prayer life, perhaps incorporating some of the practices you have explored in this study guide. Identify any of the prayers from the Old Testament that you would like to memorize, and write them out on a piece of paper to keep with you or post somewhere easily visible in your home or office. You could use a prayer from the Bible as a screensaver on your computer, or you could tape a prayer on the mirror in your bathroom. The prayers in the Bible can be a rich companion to our own personal prayers.

Leader's Notes

Leading a Bible discussion can be an enjoyable and rewarding experience. But it can also be scary especially if you've never done it before. If this is your feeling, you're in good company. When God asked Moses to lead the Israelites out of Egypt, he replied, "O Lord, please send someone else to do it!" (Ex 4:13). It was the same with Solomon, Jeremiah and Timothy, but God helped these people in spite of their weaknesses, and he will help you as well.

You don't need to be an expert on the Bible or a trained teacher to lead a Bible discussion. The idea behind these inductive studies is that the leader guides group members to discover for themselves what the Bible has to say. This method of learning will allow group members to remember much more of what is said than a lecture would.

These studies are designed to be led easily. As a matter of fact, the flow of questions through the passage from observation to interpretation to application is so natural that you may feel that the studies lead themselves. This study guide is also flexible. You can use it with a variety of groups student, professional, neighborhood or church groups. Each study takes forty-five to sixty minutes in a group setting.

There are some important facts to know about group dynamics and encouraging discussion. The suggestions listed below should enable you to effectively and enjoyably fulfill your role as leader.

Preparing for the Study

1. Ask God to help you understand and apply the passage in your own life. Unless this happens, you will not be prepared to lead others. Pray too for the various members of the group. Ask God to open your hearts to the message of his Word and motivate you to action.

2. Read the introduction to the entire guide to get an overview of the entire book and the issues which will be explored.

3. As you begin each study, read and reread the assigned Bible passage to familiarize yourself with it.

4. This study guide is based on the New International Version of the Bible. It will help you and the group if you use this translation as the basis for your study and discussion.

5. Carefully work through each question in the study. Spend time in meditation and reflection as you consider how to respond.

6. Write your thoughts and responses in the space provided in the study guide. This will help you to express your understanding of the passage clearly.

7. It might help to have a Bible dictionary handy. Use it to look up any unfamiliar words, names or places. (For additional help on how to study a passage, see chapter five of *How to Lead a LifeBuilder Study*, IVP, 2018.)

8. Consider how you can apply the Scripture to your life. Remember that the group will follow your lead in responding to the studies. They will not go any deeper than you do.

9. Once you have finished your own study of the passage, familiarize yourself with the leader's notes for the study you are leading. These are designed to help you in several ways. First, they tell you the purpose the study guide author had in mind when writing the study. Take time to think through how the study questions work together to accomplish that purpose. Second, the notes provide you with additional background information or suggestions on group dynamics for various questions. This information can be useful when people have difficulty under-standing or answering a question. Third, the leader's notes can alert you to potential problems you may encounter during the study.

10. If you wish to remind yourself of anything mentioned in the leader's notes, make a note to yourself below that question in the study.

Leading the Study

1. Begin the study on time. Open with prayer, asking God to help the group to understand and apply the passage.

2. Be sure that everyone in your group has a study guide. Encour-age the group to prepare beforehand for each discussion by reading the introduction to the guide and by working through the questions in the study.

3. At the beginning of your first time together, explain that these studies are meant to be discussions, not lectures. Encourage the members of the group to participate. However, do not put pressure on those who may be hesitant to speak during the first few sessions. You may want to suggest the following guidelines to your group.

☐ Stick to the topic being discussed.

☐ Your responses should be based on the verses which are the focus of the discussion and not on outside authorities such as commentaries or speakers.

☐ These studies focus on a particular passage of Scripture. Only rarely should you refer to other portions of the Bible. This allows for everyone to participate in in-depth study on equal ground.

☐ Anything said in the group is considered confidential and will not be discussed outside the group unless specific permission is given to do so.

☐ We will listen attentively to each other and provide time for each person present to talk.

☐ We will pray for each other.

4. Have a group member read the introduction at the beginning of the discussion.

5. Every session begins with a group discussion question. The question or activity is meant to be used before the passage is read. The question introduces the theme of the study and encourages group members to begin to open up. Encourage as many members as possible to participate, and be ready to get the discussion going with your own response.

This section is designed to reveal where our thoughts or feelings need to be transformed by Scripture. That is why it is especially important not to read the passage before the discussion question is asked. The passage will tend to color the honest reactions people would otherwise give because they are, of course, supposed to think the way the Bible does.

You may want to supplement the group discussion question with an icebreaker to help people to get comfortable. See the community section of the *Small Group Starter Kit* (IVP, 1995) for more ideas.

You also might want to use the personal reflection question with your group. Either allow a time of silence for people to respond individually or discuss it together.

6. Have a group member (or members if the passage is long) read aloud the passage to be studied. Then give people several minutes to read the passage again silently so that they can take it all in.

7. Question 1 will generally be an overview question designed to briefly survey the passage. Encourage the group to look at the whole passage, but try to avoid getting sidetracked by questions or issues that will be addressed later in the study.

8. As you ask the questions, keep in mind that they are designed to be used just as they are written. You may simply read them aloud. Or you may prefer to express them in your own words.

There may be times when it is appropriate to deviate from the study guide. For example, a question may have already been answered. If so, move on to the next question. Or someone may raise an important question not covered in the guide. Take time to discuss it, but try to keep the group from going off on tangents.

9. Avoid answering your own questions. If necessary, repeat or re-phrase them until they are clearly understood. Or point out something you read in the leader's notes to clarify the context or meaning. An eager group quickly becomes passive and silent if they think the leader will do most of the talking.

10. Don't be afraid of silence. People may need time to think about the question before formulating their answers.

11. Don't be content with just one answer. ask, "What do the rest of you think?" or "Anything else?" until several people have given answers to the question.

12. Acknowledge all contributions. Try to be affirming whenever possible. Never reject an answer. If it is clearly off-base, ask, "Which verse led you to that conclusion?" or again, "What do the rest of you think?"

13. Don't expect every answer to be addressed to you, even though this will probably happen at first. As group members become more at ease, they will begin to truly interact with each other. This is one sign of healthy discussion.

14. Don't be afraid of controversy. It can be very stimulating. If you don't resolve an issue completely, don't be frustrated. Move on and keep it in mind for later. A subsequent study may solve the problem.

15. Periodically summarize what the group has said about the passage. This helps to draw together the various ideas mentioned and gives continuity to the study. But don't preach.

16. At the end of the Bible discussion you may want to allow group members a time of quiet to work on an idea under "Now or Later." Then discuss what you experienced. Or you may want to encourage group members to work on these ideas between meetings. Give an opportunity during the session for people to talk about what they are learning.

17. Conclude your time together with conversational prayer, adapting the prayer suggestion at the end of the study to your group. Ask for God's help in following through on the commitments you've made.

18. End on time.

Many more suggestions and helps are found in *How to Lead a LifeBuilder Study.*

Components of Small Groups

A healthy small group should do more than study the Bible. There are four components to consider as you structure your time together.

Nurture. Small groups help us to grow in our knowledge and love of God. Bible study is the key to making this happen and is the foundation of your small group.

Community. Small groups are a great place to develop deep friendships with other Christians. Allow time for informal interaction before and after each study. Plan activities and games that will help you get to know each other. Spend time having fun together going on a picnic or cooking dinner together.

Worship and prayer. Your study will be enhanced by spending time praising God together in prayer or song. Pray for each other's needs and keep track of how God is answering prayer in your group. Ask God to help you to apply what you are learning in your study.

Outreach. Reaching out to others can be a practical way of applying what you are learning, and it will keep your group from becoming self-focused. Host a series of evangelistic discussions for your friends or neighbors. Clean up the yard of an elderly friend. Serve at a soup kitchen together, or spend a day working in the community.

Many more suggestions and helps in each of these areas are found in the *Small Group Starter Kit.* You will also find information on building a small group. Reading through the starter kit will be worth your time.

Study 1. A Prayer of Moses. Exodus 15:1-18.

Purpose: To grow in our intentionality in expressing praise, thanks and celebration in prayer.

General note. Exodus 1—14 describes the slavery of the Israelites in Egypt, the calling of Moses to serve his people and the way God used a series of plagues to free the Israelites. This story of release from slavery is central to the Israelites' understanding of who they are and who God is, and it lays the foundation for the life, death and resurrection of Jesus, who freed us from slavery to sin and death.

Question 2. Adele Ahlberg Calhoun, in the *Spiritual Disciplines Handbook*, defines celebration as taking "joyful, passionate pleasure in God and the radically glorious nature of God's people, Word, world and purposes" ([Downers Grove, Ill.: InterVarsity Press, 2006], p. 26). We can grow in taking joyful pleasure in God by finding new vocabulary that clearly and vividly expresses some of the ways God acts in our lives. Perhaps Moses' prayer will provide some of that new vocabulary for you.

Question 5. In Moses' time, the countries in the area around Israel practiced polytheism, worshiping numerous gods who were believed to perform different functions. Israel was unique in worshiping only one God. Israel's God combined majesty and glory with the willingness to work wonders for the people because of his tender care for them.

Question 6. The nations mentioned in verses 14 to 16 are close to Egypt, so the news of the destruction of Pharaoh's army would have spread to them, and they would have contact with the Israelites in the years to come. The Philistines lived in the part of Palestine that bordered Egypt and would have been first to hear of the exodus. The Israelites would journey to Edom and Moab in the next forty years. Canaan is the whole region into which Israel would later settle.

Question 10. We need to remember two aspects of God's actions in our lives: the actions that are specific to us, and the actions of God that show his care for all people. To help remember the ways God has acted specifically in our own lives, many people find a prayer journal to be helpful. Taking time every day, perhaps at bedtime, to look back over the day to thank God for his actions in our lives can also be helpful. Reading Scripture is one of the most helpful ways to remember what God has done for all people, because God as Creator, Redeemer and Sustainer is revealed over and over in the pages of the Bible.

Study 2. A Prayer of Hannah. 1 Samuel 2:1-10.

Purpose: To grow in openness to praying for unexpected and impossible things.

Group discussion. Be sure to have pieces of paper and pencils or pens for the participants to use.

General note. Hannah's story of infertility, her prayer to God for a child and God's answer to her prayer is told in 1 Samuel 1. Hannah's prayer of thankfulness for her son goes far beyond a focus on that birth. Walter Brueggemann writes, "While the newborn son is celebrated, the song finally concerns not the son but Yahweh. The accent is on the Giver, not the gift. Precious as the gift is, the Giver is the one who outruns Israel's awed expectations. Praise is the only speech appropriate to the occasion" (*First and Second Samuel* [Louisville, Ky.: John Knox, 1990], p. 16).

Question 1. "Horn" in the Old Testament literally meant the horn of the ram and the wild ox. Horns were used as musical instruments and as a receptacle for oil used for anointing. The word "horn" is also used metaphorically in the Old Testament in two ways, either of which could be relevant to its use in verse 1. The altar used for sacrifices had protuberances on the four corners that were called horns. The sacrificial blood was smeared on the horns of the altar, so the horns were viewed as a place of refuge. Horns also symbolized power. In verse 1, either power or refuge makes sense for the metaphorical use of "horn."

Question 3. Fertility was a central focus for women in Hannah's time, so Hannah has undoubtedly felt some criticism from her family members and friends because she has been unable to conceive a child. We know that Peninah, Hannah's husband's other wife, taunted Hannah for her infertility (see 1 Sam 1:6-7). Perhaps in her prayer Hannah is trying to counter some of the things people have said to her, so in a sense she might be speaking to them even though they are not present. Or perhaps she is speaking to herself, saying words that refute the inner shame she has felt because of her failure to conceive. Or perhaps she is speaking to God throughout the passage, even though she is using third person for much of it, in the same way that we sing about God in praise songs and hymns.

Question 6. A prayer from the Gallican Sacramentary (France, fifth to ninth century) expresses concern for people in need in a similar way to Hannah's prayer. This gentle prayer reads: "O God, the author of love and the lover of pure peace and affection: let all who are terrified by fears, afflicted by poverty, harassed by tribulation, worn down by illness, be set free by your indulgent tenderness, raised up by amendment of life and cherished by your daily compassion" (Thomas C. Oden and Cindy Crosby, eds., *Ancient Christian Devotional* [Downers Grove, Ill.: IVP Books, 2007], p. 150). The beautiful words of this ancient prayer can apply to ourselves, as well as to others, in time of need, because the prayer affirms God's deep tenderness and concern for people in any kind of pain or trouble.

Question 8. The last two lines of the prayer talk about the king. Hannah prayed this prayer at the end of the period of the judges, when Israel had no king. Hannah's child, Samuel, grew up to be the prophet who anointed Israel's first two kings, Solomon and David. So the prayer contains a foreshadowing of the kings who would be anointed by Samuel. In fact, in some ways David's life is an example of the kinds of reversals in Hannah's prayer. David was the eighth son of a poor family, the last person anyone would expect to be king. His battle with Goliath is an example of a mighty warrior who is defeated by a seemingly insignificant opponent.

Question 9. Hannah's prayer reflects a complete flip-flop of the social order. It is one of the most radical parts of the Bible. In her prayer, the mighty become weak, the feeble become strong, the wealthy become hungry, and the poor become fat. Hannah sees clearly that this flip-flop applies to her own life, while also describing God's care for others in need. God is at work changing social patterns, so it is not personal strength that ultimately enables a person to triumph.

Question 10. This combination—God's power and God's willingness to enter into our world—has been understood for generations as a central theme of the gospel, most evident in Jesus Christ. A traditional Advent prayer expresses this theme: "Stir up your power, O Lord, and with great might come among us; and, because we are sorely hindered by our sins, let your bountiful grace and mercy speedily help and deliver us; through Jesus Christ our Lord, to whom, with you and the Holy Spirit, be honor and glory, now and for ever. Amen" (Book of Common Prayer [New York: The Church Hymnal Corporation, 1979], p. 212).

Study 3. A Prayer of Samuel. 1 Samuel 3:1-14.

Purpose: To become more willing to try to listen to God in prayer.

General note. After he was weaned, Hannah left her son to be raised by Eli, the priest in the house of the Lord at Shiloh. This was in response to the vow Hannah made when she prayed to get pregnant (1 Sam 1:9-11). Scholars don't know what age children were weaned at in ancient Israel, and this story doesn't give any clues to Samuel's age.

Question 2. This story takes place in the time of the judges, before Israel had a king. In fact, the child in this story, Samuel, grows up to be the prophet who anoints the first two kings of Israel. Jerusalem had not yet become the capital of Israel and the temple in Jerusalem had not yet been built. The ark of the covenant, viewed as the place where God's presence dwelled on earth, was at Shiloh, about twenty miles north of Jerusalem, in a building often called "the house of the LORD," although in this passage it is called the temple. Up until this time, the main way that God spoke to people was through visions.

Question 4. The lamps in Samuel and Eli's time used olive oil or animal fat and a wick, and they could burn for two to four hours. If the lamp was still burning, it is likely that this story took place just a few hours after nightfall.

Question 6. Joyce Huggett, in *The Joy of Listening to God*, describes her own personal journey of learning to listen to God. She noticed two significant problems that impeded her ability to hear God: first, being too busy to stop and listen, and second, being unwilling to obey God. She reflects, "I wanted the best of both worlds: my way and God's" ([Downers Grove, Ill.: InterVarsity Press, 1987], p. 167).

Question 7. Remember that Hannah prayed in 1 Samuel 2:1-10 about things being turned upside down. Here is one manifestation of the way God does that. Eli is the priest, Samuel is a child. Yet the child is the one to whom God speaks, and this child grows up to be a greater leader than Eli was.

Question 8. In the Hebrew language and worldview, to listen to someone or to hear someone implied an intention to act on the words. Today we separate listening from acting; we hear people say things, but we don't necessarily do anything about what we hear. "Speak, LORD, for your servant is listening" meant that the person speaking those words was willing to do what God asked.

Question 10. Marjorie J. Thompson, in *Soul Feast: An Invitation to the Christian Spiritual Life*, describes the ways Christians hear God speak: first and foremost through Scripture, but also in nature, through one another, through circumstances of life, in dreams, through journal keeping and in an inner certainty ([Louisville, Ky.: Westminster John Knox, 1995], pp. 33-36). All of these require some form of making space in our lives to focus on God. It takes time to read the Bible and journal. Careful reflection is required to discern God's voice through circumstances, relationships with others, dreams and an inner certainty.

Study 4. A Prayer of Solomon. 1 Kings 8:22-53.

Purpose: To learn to pray for our nation and other nations with a heart for God's priorities.

Question 2. In this passage, Solomon may be referring to two different promises made by God, first to the nation of Israel and second to Solomon's father, David. In Deuteronomy 7:9-12, God promises to be faithful to the people of Israel if they follow him. In 2 Samuel 7:12-13, God promises David, through the words of the prophet Nathan, that his son would be the one to build a temple for God. These promises give Solomon the confidence to pray with assurance, knowing that God truly cares about the well-being of the nation of Israel. Learning God's promises from the Bible can help us pray with confidence for the needs in our world today.

Question 3. Christians often use the language of transcendence and immanence to address the question of where God dwells. Richard D. Nelson writes, "Chapter 8 affirms both transcendence and immanence simultaneously. . . . God is 'really present' in the temple in cloud, glory and ark (vv. 3-13). Yet lest this be understood as suggesting that God is automatically at Israel's beck and call, Solomon insists that even the whole universe cannot contain God" (*First and Second Kings,* Interpretation [Atlanta: John Knox Press, 1987], p. 59).

This section of Solomon's prayer is fascinating because it takes place before Christ came to earth, yet Solomon is speaking about the fact that even though God dwells in heaven, God loves us enough to be present on earth in some sense as well. God became fully present on earth in Jesus Christ, and after Jesus' death and resurrection, the Holy Spirit was sent to us to continue to be God's presence on earth. So today we affirm that God lives both in heaven and on earth.

Question 6. Solomon sees a natural progression, described in verses 41 and 42. God has done wonderful things for the nation of Israel. This news of God's goodness and power will certainly spread around the world, Solomon believes, and people in other nations will understandably want to come to the place where this amazing God is worshiped. He welcomes the idea that foreigners will come and worship because their desire to come will result from God's good reputation among the nations, and what they learn about God from their visit to the temple will cause the further spread of knowledge about this wonderful God after they return home.

Question 7. Solomon's prayer for foreigners as they pray in the temple reflects tenderness for the individuals who pray, as well as strategic thinking about the spread of the good news about God's power and goodness around the world. This combination that Solomon expresses—tender care for individuals as well as desire for the spread of the knowledge of God—is a wonderful combination to keep in mind when praying for the needs of people who don't yet know God.

Question 9. The word *servant* is a common word in the Old Testament with a variety of meanings. It can refer to slaves, hired workers and personal attendants. Officials are referred to as servants of the king, and kings as servants of the people. "Your servant" can be used to refer to oneself in a humble way. Common themes in most of the uses of *servant* are humility, helping, respect and obedience. Solomon's reference to himself as God's servant evokes his desire to put God's priorities ahead of his own in his words and actions.

Question 10. One of the prayers of Patrick of Ireland (c. 389-481) has some of the same themes as Solomon's prayer, even though it is much shorter. I can imagine a leader praying Patrick's prayer for a public occasion: "We bind ourselves to you today, you our God: your power to hold us, your hand to guide us, your word to give us speech, your presence to defend us, this day and every day; in the name of the blessed Trinity, Father, Son and Holy Spirit, to whom be the kingdom, and the power, and the glory, forever and ever. Amen" (Oden and Crosby, *Ancient Christian Devotional*, p. 87).

Question 11. Here are two examples of prayers that are structured like Solomon's: "When earthquakes and tsunamis strike around the world, and victims pray to you for help in their great need, will you please motivate people to send aid, and may your love and care be revealed through the Christians who distribute that aid." "When HIV/AIDS spreads to innocent children, will you please provide medical care for those children, and will you motivate Christians to tell those children of your great love for them?"

Study 5. A Prayer of Isaiah. Isaiah 6.

Purpose: To grow in willingness to be commissioned by God.

Question 2. Scholars believe King Uzziah died sometime between 740 and 735 B.C. The death of the king may be significant in indicating that the nation of Israel was in turmoil and mourning because of the king's death, and a prophet would be needed to help the nation remember that the fate of the nation rests in God's hands. In addition, giving a date conveys a sense of concreteness, making the event seem more real and indicating that the event really did happen at a particular time in history.

Question 3. The Old Testament teaches that to see God is to die (Gen 32:30; Ex 19:21; 33:20; Deut 18:16). Yet a few individuals got to see God and live. Exodus 24, for example, records that Moses, Aaron, Nadab, Abihu and the seventy elders saw God; the most they could describe, however, was the pavement under his feet, which was made of sapphire (Ex 24:10). The fact that creatures seldom get to look directly at their Creator probably explains why the seraphs cover their eyes in God's presence.

The threefold repetition of "holy" is significant. In the Hebrew world, repeating something three times indicates it is the ultimate of that characteristic, so saying God is holy three times indicates that nothing is more holy than God. The meaning of holiness has two components, both of which are visible in this passage. Something that is holy is separate from everyday use, and Isaiah's vision shows the utter otherness of God. In addition, holiness when referring to God conveys moral purity, and Isaiah's response indicates that God's moral purity was very clear to him.

Question 4. John N. Oswalt describes Isaiah's reaction: "For the finite, the mortal, the incomplete, and the fallible to encounter the Infinite, the Eternal, the Self-consistent, and the Infallible is to know the futility and hopelessness of one's existence. . . . But it is not the recognition of his finitude that crushes Isaiah; it is his uncleanness. The primary element about God's holiness that distinguishes him from human beings is not his essence but his character" (*The Book of Isaiah: Chapters 1-39* [Grand Rapids: Eerdmans, 1986], pp. 182-83).

Question 5. In the Hebrew mindset, the mouth speaks what is in the heart. Jesus reflects this reality in Mark 7:15.

Question 9. Verses 9-10 are extremely hard to interpret. Commentators have various ways of explaining what these verses mean, and most commentators indicate their difficulty with these verses. Jesus alludes to these verses in Luke 8:10 and quotes them in the parable of the sower in Mark 4:12 and Matthew 13:13-15. The idea in the parable of the sower seems to be that it's better for people not to respond to God at all than for them to respond in a superficial way that has no depth. So God may close the ears, eyes and hearts of people as an act of mercy to prevent them from an insincere response to him.

Question 11. "Seed" in the Old Testament can refer to offspring or descendants. So this verse could refer to the continuation of the nation of Israel after it is cut down like a tree. Yes, God says, there will still be descendants, a remnant who will live, and the nation will survive. The holy seed could also refer to Jesus, who will be born from within the nation of Israel, and will bring salvation to the nation of Israel and the people of the whole earth.

Study 6. A Prayer of Jeremiah. Jeremiah 20.

Purpose: To grow in willingness to bring every emotion to God.

Question 2. The kind of stocks used in Jeremiah's time forced the body into an awkward, bent position. In fact, the Hebrew word for stocks has the root meaning "distort." The awkward position would add physical discomfort to the shame of being disciplined publicly.

Question 3. Jeremiah prophesied for almost forty years, between 626 and 587 B.C., when Jerusalem fell to the Babylonians and all of its people were carted off into exile. Jeremiah's prophecies came true in 587, and the other prophets who said that all would be well were proved to be wrong. But forty years is a long time to wait for a prophecy to be fulfilled. And during those forty years Jeremiah received almost no positive reward for his obedience to God.

Question 4. Jeremiah's situation regarding God's word and his own words is described by Jack R. Lundbom: "Jeremiah says that speaking Yahweh's word has brought him nothing but derision. It is ongoing—all day, day after day! He considered keeping silent, which may be what people were telling him to do and doubtless what they wished he would do, but that brought him no peace. In fact, Yahweh's word within him was like a burning fire, imprisoned, wanting to get out. Try as he might, he was unable to keep it in. This was his dilemma: Damned if he speaks; damned if he doesn't. There is no solution; no way to achieve peace" (*Jeremiah 1-20: A New Translation with Introduction and Commentary* [New York: Doubleday, 1999], p. 858).

Question 5. Walter Brueggemann writes concerning this passage, "How honest the Bible is! It does not deny or deceive about how costly the truth of God's word is. Such deep faith as Jeremiah's does not lead neatly to well-being, but to recurring crisis. The Bible knows about troubled, bitter faith that is left resolved." Brueggemann goes on to point out that Jeremiah, no matter how overwhelmed with pain, remains faithful to God and never curses God (*To Pluck Up, To Tear Down: A Commentary on the Book of Jeremiah 1-25* [Grand Rapids: Eerdmans, 1988], p. 178).

Question 6. When God called Jeremiah to be a prophet in the first chapter of the book, God makes the same promise two times to Jeremiah: "I am with you and will rescue you" (Jer 1:8, repeated in 1:19). This promise seems to lie behind the words Jeremiah says about God in verses 11 to 13 of chapter 20.

Question 10. Many Christians find that journaling is a helpful practice for growing in honesty before God. Journaling provides the opportunity to ask hard questions of God and to write down honest emotions. Those questions and emotions can be turned into prayers that are silent, spoken or written down in the journal. Other possibilities for growing in honesty before God include a prayer partner or prayer support group, which can create a place for honest sharing that flows into honest prayers. Praying the psalms—reading the psalms slowly enough to make them our own prayers—is another practice that can nurture openness about our emotions and help us learn to pray honestly about how we feel. Many diverse emotions are recorded in the psalms, and the psalm writers bring all those emotions to God.

Study 7. A Prayer of Jonah. Jonah 2.

Purpose: To grow in resting in God as our salvation, so we can pray in challenging situations.

Question 2. Verse 2 is written in the past tense, as if God has already delivered Jonah. Yet the prayer takes place from the belly of the fish, before God has rescued Jonah. This reflects an amazing level of faith, particularly because Jonah's disobedience landed him in the predicament in the first place.

Question 5. Jonah's prayer follows a prayer structure commonly found in the Old Testament called a lament. A lament typically includes a word of teaching. It is interesting to ponder whether verse 8 summarizes the lesson a person might learn from a situation like Jonah's.

Question 6. "Worthless idols" can also be translated "false vanities," which is another way to describe the things that get us off track and draw us away from God. The worthless idols and false vanities of our time are often connected to excessive striving for money, possessions, job success, physical beauty and social status.

"Grace" here is the word that is often translated "steadfast love." It's worth spending some time pondering the ways that worthless idols and false vanities turn our focus away from God's grace and steadfast love. Every unit of energy we spend chasing worthless things is a unit of energy we aren't putting toward prayer, trust in God and growing in faith.

Question 9. Basil the Great, bishop of Caesarea in the fourth century, wrote a prayer that reflects an awareness that only God is our salvation: "Almighty God, who sees that we have no power of ourselves to help ourselves: Keep us, both outwardly in our bodies and inwardly in our souls, that we may be defended from all adversities which may happen to the body and from all evil thoughts which may assault and hurt the soul; through Jesus Christ our Lord. Amen" (Oden and Crosby, *Ancient Christian Devotional*, p. 95).

Study 8. A Prayer of Habakkuk. Habakkuk 3.
Purpose: To grow in learning to pray from a position of trust in all situations.
General note. Scholars are not sure of the meaning of "On *shigionoth*" (v. 1) and "*Selah*" (vv. 3, 9, 13). They may refer to instructions regarding instruments or the way music is played, which raises the possibility that this prayer of Habakkuk might have been set to music for corporate worship.
Question 1. God's power in nature is a theme of Habakkuk's prayer. In addition, Habakkuk may be remembering God's deeds in Israel's history. Teman (v. 3) was in Edom, to the south and a little bit east of Israel (in what is now Jordan). Mount Paran (v. 3) was located south of Israel, just north of Mount Sinai. Cushan (v. 7) probably refers to the area south of Egypt, and Midian (also in v. 7) is located south of Edom on the east side of the Gulf of Aqaba (in what is now Saudi Arabia). These locations evoke many incidents from Exodus and Joshua. The plagues and pestilence of verse 5 probably refer to the ten plagues in Egypt (Ex 5—12). The sea and the victorious chariots in verse 8 and the churning of the great waters in verse 15 probably refer to the crossing of the Red Sea (Ex 14), as well as the crossing of the Jordan River (Josh 3).
Question 4. "Decay crept into my bones" refers to feeling weak and limp. J. H. Eaton writes about the impact of the vision on Habakkuk: "Under the strong hand of God, the prophet trembles and totters and feels as if his body were disintegrating. While revelation itself may be overpowering, for Habakkuk it is even more the awful content of his vision which causes him to groan. He has glimpsed the advent of God, and though its goal is salvation, it must first bring upheavals altogether terrifying to the frail human seer" (*Obadiah, Nahum, Habakkuk, and Zephaniah: Introduction and Commentary* [London: SCM Press, 1961], p. 116).
Question 5. Habakkuk's statement that he will wait for calamity to come upon the nation invading Israel is an affirmation that he has heard what God said earlier. God is going to judge the people of Israel for their disobedience by bringing the Babylonians to destroy them, but the Babylonians will later receive judgment for their own fierce destructive power. "Jeremiah and Habakkuk were contemporaries: Jeremiah taught that

wickedness in God's own people is doomed; Habakkuk, that wickedness in the [Babylonians], also, is doomed. Tyranny always carries within it the seeds of its own destruction" (George L. Robinson, *The Twelve Minor Prophets* [New York: George H. Doran Company, 1926], p. 127). For Habakkuk, God's answer changed his perspective because he saw that the tyrants of his time would themselves be destroyed. Habakkuk's prayer affirms that he is willing to let God work out his purposes in time, and that he is willing to trust that God oversees human history and will bring justice in the end.

Question 7. Think about the kinds of "big" situations today in which people find it hard to trust God: difficulties at work or difficulties finding a job, financial struggles, health issues, the death of loved ones, estrangement from family members and friends, living far away from family and friends, and many other kinds of losses. But think also about the "small" daily frustrations that cause stress. Be specific as you come up with your answer. Here's an example: "Even though my checkbook balance is lower than I like, even though my boss has been irritable lately, even though my son forgot Mother's Day . . . yet I will rejoice in the Lord."

Question 8. One of the most helpful ways to rejoice in God in the midst of difficult circumstances is to practice thankfulness. This requires paying attention to the ways God is answering prayers, even if the major difficulty is not resolved. For example, when a family member has cancer, it may be possible to thank God for the clear explanations a doctor has given, the kindness of a nurse, a mild reaction to the drugs instead of a severe response, an understanding boss, a reliable car, the support of friends who are praying and giving practical help, etc. Even having food on the table is a blessing in the midst of a crisis, when we pause and remember that many people in crisis around the world are dealing with an empty pantry as well as whatever the crisis happens to be. God is always working in our lives, even in very hard times, but we are often so focused on the major problem at hand that we don't take the time to notice and give thanks for the multitude of ways God cares for us.

Question 9. Deer are sure-footed on steep, rocky or dangerous terrain. Often they are able to sprint across uneven ground where humans would find walking difficult. This provides a vivid and encouraging picture of people of faith who move sure-footedly through difficult territory because of their confidence in God's help. The picture of a deer bounding—or perhaps just walking!—across an uneven hillside can provide a mental image of God's strength and guidance in difficult times.

Question 11. Many people engage in practices that help them place their struggles into God's hands. I often imagine Jesus standing beside a big cross. I walk toward him in my imagination and I give my troubles into his hands or I lay them at his feet.

I also find breath prayer helpful. As I breathe in, I imagine myself breathing in God's love and mercy. When I breathe out, I imagine that I am breathing out my concerns into God's presence and care.

Sabbath keeping is another spiritual practice that has helped me grow in trusting God, because on that day of rest I experience the reality that God is taking care of the universe when I am not being productive.

Lynne M. Baab is the author of the Prayers of the New Testament *and* Sabbath *LifeBuilder Bible Studies as well as numerous books, including* Fasting, Sabbath Keeping *and* Reaching Out in a Networked World. *A Presbyterian minister, she completed a PhD in communication at the University of Washington in 2007 and moved with her husband to Dunedin, New Zealand, where she taught pastoral theology at the University of Otago for ten years. She returned to her home city, Seattle, in 2017 and still supervises graduate students for her university in New Zealand.*